EVOLVING TECHNOLOGY

THE EVOLUTION OF MEDICAL TECHNOLOGY

HILLARY DODGE

Britannica®
Educational Publishing
IN ASSOCIATION WITH
ROSEN
EDUCATIONAL SERVICES

Published in 2019 by Britannica Educational Publishing (a trademark of Encyclopædia Britannica, Inc.) in association with The Rosen Publishing Group, Inc.
29 East 21st Street, New York, NY 10010

Distributed exclusively by Rosen Publishing.
To see additional Britannica Educational Publishing titles, go to rosenpublishing.com.

First Edition

Britannica Educational Publishing
J.E. Luebering: Executive Director, Core Editorial
Andrea R. Field: Managing Editor, Compton's by Britannica

Rosen Publishing
Bailey Maxim: Editor
Nelson Sá: Art Director
Brian Garvey: Series Designer
Tahara Anderson: Book Layout
Cindy Reiman: Photography Manager
Ellina Litmanovich: Photo Researcher

Library of Congress Cataloging-in-Publication Data

Names: Dodge, Hillary, author.
Title: The evolution of medical technology / Hillary Dodge.
Description: New York : Britannica Educational Publishing, in Association with Rosen Educational Services, 2019. | Series: Evolving technology | Includes bibliographical references and index. | Audience: Grades 5–8.
Identifiers: LCCN 2017048763| ISBN 9781538303245 (library bound : alk. paper) | ISBN 9781538303252 (pbk. : alk. paper)
Subjects: LCSH: Medicine—History—Juvenile literature. | Medical innovations—History—Juvenile literature. | Medical technology—Juvenile literature.
Classification: LCC R133.5 .D63 2019 | DDC 610.9—dc23
LC record available at https://lccn.loc.gov/2017048763

Manufactured in the United States of America

CONTENTS

INTRODUCTION

It's hard to imagine life without antibiotics or yearly visits to the doctor. But there was a time when doctor visits were rare events, undertaken only in the direst of emergencies. It is only through the evolving efforts of thinkers, physicians, and scientists over the course of human history that we have the medical industry we rely upon today.

Modern medical knowledge has deep roots that originated with the earliest civilizations. Medicine advanced as human understanding of science grew over time. The ancient Egyptians were among the first to use herbs and plant-based substances to treat illness. In medieval times, Christian monks studied medicinal uses for the plants they tended in monastery gardens. The invention of the compound microscope in the sixteenth century allowed scientists for the first time to actually see the smallest parts of the human body. This brought a new understanding of the workings of the body, as well as of the microorganisms that cause illness.

Knowledge of the unseen world and the medicinal benefits of plants allowed scientists over time to develop increasingly sophisticated medicines that could heal and even eradicate certain diseases. Similar stories apply to other fields in modern medicine.

From surgery to general practice to pathology, modern medicine today rests on a foundation of knowledge that stretches back over centuries.

The practice of medicine—the science and art of preventing, alleviating, and curing disease—is one of the oldest professional callings. Since ancient times, healers with varying degrees of knowledge and skills have sought to restore the health or relieve the distress of the sick and injured. Often, that meant doing little more than offering sympathy to the patient while nature took its course. Today, however, practitioners of medicine have several millennia of medical advances on which to base their care of patients.

The earliest doctors were tribal healers or shamans. As civilization developed, healers evolved into thinkers and philosophers who tried to understand the world around them. During the Middle Ages, the church took over the role of healing, ascribing a spiritual component to the process. By the Renaissance, however, science and medicine veered away from religious structure and turned again toward rational inquiry. Medical schools were established to further medical study.

Dissection and experimentation were central to the medical studies during the Industrial Revolution

Thanks to a long history of medical discovery and innovation, today's hospitals and medical centers are large and well-equipped.

and early twentieth century. As medical knowledge and technology expanded, physicians began to use a form of deductive reasoning that came to be called the scientific method. Data from studies using the scientific method resulted in more accurate identifications and promising theories.

Today, physicians are the key health care providers in most developed countries. In order to practice medicine, all medical practitioners must meet rigorous educational, professional, and ethical standards before they become licensed to treat patients. They undergo intensive schooling and in many cases undertake postgraduate training to expand their skills.

The story of medical innovation and the technology devised to combat injury and illness is rife with challenges and victories. With the vast knowledge of the millennia as a foundation, medical practice and the technology that supports it continue to expand, improving human life and well-being.

ANCIENT MEDICINE

Humankind's desire to know more about the human body stretches back across human history. Evidence of attempts to care for the sick and injured predates written records. Skulls found in Europe and South America dating as far back as 10,000 BCE have shown that the practice of trepanning—the removal of a portion of the skull bone—was not uncommon. This operation, performed by many early peoples, including American Indians, was probably done to release evil spirits that were thought to be the source of illness; yet, in many cases, it proved to be the medically correct thing to do. Opening the skull can relieve pressure and pain caused by brain tumors and head injuries.

Indeed, early people often misunderstood what caused disease, attributing illness to evil spirits, angry gods, spiritual imbalance, and even the wrongdoings of the sick person. Early medical practices involved the use of magic and incantations to ward off demons and disease. Healing rituals were performed by shamans or other spiritual leaders. It wasn't until the late Egyptian dynasties that the first physicians began to emerge with a profession apart from religion.

EGYPTIAN MEDICINE

On his visits to Egypt during the fifth century BCE, the Greek physician Herodotus noted several practices among the Egyptians that contributed to the health and well-being of their society. He observed advanced practices in hygiene and cleanliness. Egyptians washed daily and wore clean clothes. They scrubbed their drinking cups and shaved their bodies to prevent infestations with lice. They linked diet to health. Additionally, Herodotus noted the growing number of specialist physicians who focused on individual ailments or parts of the body.

Ancient Egyptian medicine was also known for its practices of bone-setting, massage, and the use of prostheses—fabricated body parts used to replace limbs lost to accident or disease. One of the best-known examples of an Egyptian prosthesis is a strap-on toe now owned by the British Museum in London. However, because prostheses were expensive they were only available to the upper classes.

The ancient Egyptians were among the first to use certain herbs and drugs, including castor oil, senna, and opium. They were reputed to be skilled diagnos-

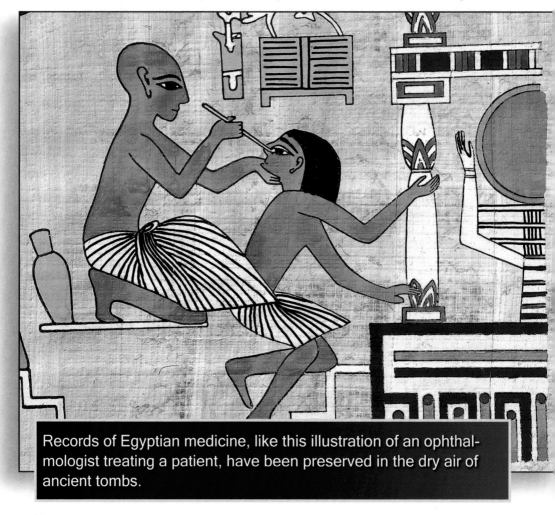

Records of Egyptian medicine, like this illustration of an ophthalmologist treating a patient, have been preserved in the dry air of ancient tombs.

ticians and kept careful records in the form of papyrus scrolls. One papyrus dated to around 3000 BCE described fifty-eight sick patients, of whom forty-two were given specific diagnoses. One of the oldest medical texts is the Ebers Papyrus, which contains roughly seven hundred magical formulas and a surprisingly accurate description of the circulatory system.

EARLY GREEK MEDICINE

Like the Egyptians, the ancient Greeks strove to understand the workings of the human body. Hippocrates, one of the best-known physicians of his time, rejected the notion that disease was punishment sent by the gods. He revolutionized medicine by putting forth a doctrine that attributed health and disease to four bodily humors, or fluids: blood, black bile, yellow bile, and phlegm. He believed that the humors were well balanced in a healthy person but that disturbances or imbalances in them caused disease. At that time, his humoral theory seemed highly scientific. In fact, doctors diagnosed and treated illnesses based on the four humors well into the nineteenth century. Knowing that he could not cure most diseases, Hippocrates tended to recommend conservative measures such as exercise, rest, and cleanliness. By contrast, for fever, which he thought was caused by an excess of blood in the body, he recommended the drastic measure of bloodletting.

Hippocrates is best known today for his ethical code (the Hippocratic Oath), which continues to be used by the medical profession as a guide to appropriate conduct. The oath is a pledge doctors make to always use their knowledge and best judgment for the benefit of their patients and to never harm or injure those in their care.

From ancient art to the modern Hippocratic Oath, Hippocrates and his medical theories have made a lasting impact upon medicine.

THE HISTORY OF BLOODLETTING

The practice of bloodletting, or phlebotomy, began many thousands of years ago. The Egyptians were its first known practitioners—the Ebers Papyrus contains the earliest written references to bloodletting. The practice was continued by the Greeks and Romans and later by physicians and healers across many cultures. It was a key element of ancient Arab medicine, which advocated a set of strict guidelines—for example, bloodletting was not recommended during a full moon or if the wind was blowing from the south. Australian Aboriginal peoples used bloodletting for pain relief. In South America, travelers

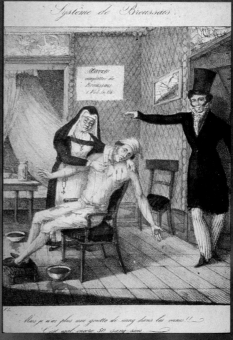

The practice of bloodletting is an artistic motif that is reproduced time and again in historical artworks; bloodletting is both a symbol of life and death.

(continued on the next page)

(continued from the previous page)

were bled to remove evil spirits or blood impurities. In more recent times bloodletting was used to manage disease outbreaks. During the American Civil War, many military doctors used it to attempt to control the spread of infectious disease.

Early tools for releasing blood from the body included sharp stones, animal bones, teeth, and even quills and thorns. The lancet, a sharp, double-edged instrument, was introduced in the fifteenth century. Other blood-collection tools used over time included cups and hollow tubes. The use of live blood-sucking leeches to remove blood dates to the first century and continued into the nineteenth century.

From the beginning, there were debates about the value of bloodletting and the appropriate amounts of blood to remove. In the early seventeenth century, physicians opposed to bloodletting released reports showing that it was often more harmful than helpful. The use of bloodletting during a cholera epidemic in the 1830s reportedly may have increased mortality by dehydrating patients. Today, bloodletting is still performed in some parts of the world.

ADVANCES IN ANATOMY

The first known systematic dissections of human bodies were conducted around 300 BCE by two Greek physician-scholars—Herophilus and Erasistratus—living in Alexandria, Egypt. They dissected virtually every organ, including the brain, and recorded what they learned. Despite their dedication to the science of anatomy, these pioneers had little influence on the subsequent practice of medicine. By 150 BCE, dissection of human cadavers was banned throughout the Hellenistic world, and any writings they left behind were lost when Alexandria's library was destroyed by fire in the third century CE.

The most significant physician of the ancient world after Hippocrates was Galen. He achieved great fame throughout the Roman Empire in the early second century. He was both a physician and a philosopher, and he also founded experimental physiology. He performed systematic experiments on animals, which involved both dissection and "vivisection," or live dissection. Galen treated wounded gladiators and took advantage of the opportunity to study the internal organs and muscles of the wounded. He recognized connections between bodily structures and functions; for example, he demonstrated that a severed spinal cord led to paralysis. He recognized that the heart circulated blood through the arteries but did not understand that it circulated in only one direction. His many writings influenced the development of medicine for 1,400 years and were partly responsible for the emergence of science in Europe during the Renaissance.

Much of what we know about Roman medicine was obtained from written records, surviving Roman art such as pottery, mosaics, and frescoes, and archaeological excavations. Knowledge of the full extent of surgical equipment used by Roman doctors remains incomplete. A large collection of instruments from the period was uncovered in Pompeii. It included bone levers, forceps, bloodletting vessels, scalpels, scissors, and probes.

OUTSIDE THE WESTERN WORLD

As medical study and practice evolved in the Roman Empire, it also flourished in other parts of the world. Ancient Chinese physicians and practitioners from the Arab and Persian worlds made great contributions that advanced medical knowledge.

In ancient Chinese medicine, qi was designated as the master force that coordinates and controls the fundamental activities of different organs in the body. In Chinese philosophy, qi is regarded as a vital energy present in the breath and the bodily fluids. Ancient theorists believed that qi flowed through the body along a system of channels, or meridians. Acupuncture, an ancient Chinese medical technique, is thought to balance different forms of energy in these channels. This allows the qi to flow freely, bringing both physical and emotional health. In addition to acupuncture, Chinese medicine used many traditional herbs, as well as meditation, to promote health.

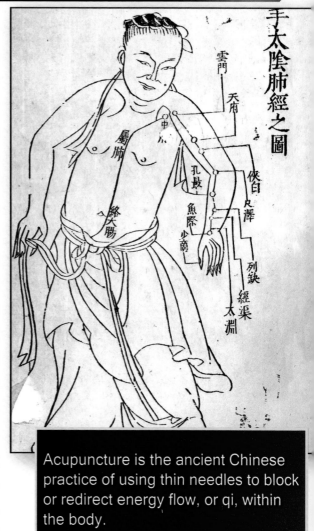

Acupuncture is the ancient Chinese practice of using thin needles to block or redirect energy flow, or qi, within the body.

After the breakup of the Roman Empire, the tradition of Greek medicine continued in the universities of the Arab world. Al-Razi, a Persian physician active around the end of the first millennium, is credited with being the first to distinguish between the highly contagious viral diseases smallpox and measles. Probably the most important physician at the beginning of the second millennium was Avicenna. His monumental *Canon of Medicine*, a five-volume encyclopedia of case histories and therapeutic instructions, was long considered an absolute medical authority in both Eastern and Western traditions.

One of the greatest achievements of the medieval Islamic world was the hospital. In contrast with the Christian monasteries of the western world, Islamic hospitals accepted and treated all persons regardless of financial status or religion. Early Islamic hospitals were large structures that served many functions—treatment and recuperation for those who were ill, safe haven for the mentally ill, and shelter for the elderly.

Chapter 2

DARK TIMES

At about the same time that the practice of medicine was flourishing in the Islamic world, the first medical school in Europe was established at Salerno, in southern Italy. Other great medieval medical schools were founded at Paris, France, and at Bologna and Padua, in Italy. However, the fall of the Roman Empire and the rise of Christianity led to a return to a view of disease and infirmity clouded by superstition and religious beliefs. Between the Middle Ages (500–1500) and the end of the Renaissance (1600), medical practice again became centered on ritual rather than science and rational thought.

LORDS AND PEASANTS

Life in the Middle Ages was difficult for everyone, though it was harder for some (namely peasants) than for others (namely lords and officials of the church). Peasant homes were incubators of disease—small, damp, and dirty, with leaky roofs, drafty windows, and muddy floors that teemed with microorganisms. Many families housed their pigs and chickens inside the home, exacerbating the unsanitary conditions. Not surprisingly, peasant villages were often beset by famines and plagues. Illness was treated by local healers who relied mainly on folk remedies.

The homes of medieval lords were very large and grand, but far from comfortable by modern standards. Manor houses were cold and drafty. Unlike the peasant families, the lord's household had a modicum of medical care. Some lords employed a private physician who resided within the manor.

Even with the presence of medical learning institutions, European medicine progressed very slowly in the Middle Ages. Medieval physicians continued to rely upon ancient medical theories, including that of the humors. They analyzed symptoms, examined waste matter, and made diagnoses. To treat illness, they might prescribe diet, rest, sleep, exercise, or baths. For some ailments they administered emetics (substances that induce vomiting) and laxatives, or they bled the patient.

Surgeons could treat fractures and dislocations, repair hernias, and perform amputations and a few other operations. Some of them prescribed opium or alcohol to deaden pain. Childbirth was left to midwives, who relied on folklore and tradition.

A DARK AGE FOR MEDICINE

The influence of the Roman Catholic Church on European medicine during the Middle Ages greatly impeded medical progress. Disease was regarded as a punishment for sin, and healing was said to require only prayer and repentance. A number of saints became associated with miraculous cures of certain diseases, such as St. Vitus for chorea (or

Many successful practices in medieval medicine were attributed to false beliefs. Drilling a hole in the skull was thought to remove evil spirits; in reality, it relieved pressure from injury.

St. Vitus's dance) and St. Anthony for erysipelas (or St. Anthony's fire). The human body was held sacred and dissection was forbidden.

Nevertheless, the medieval church played an important role in caring for the sick. Great hospitals were established during the Middle Ages by religious foundations, and infirmaries were attached to abbeys, monasteries, priories, and convents. Doctors and nurses in these institutions were members of religious orders and combined spiritual with physical healing. Many monasteries housed small hospital wards, supported by wealthy patrons and local lords. Many doctors were monks who devoted themselves to healing, much of which consisted of administering potions and praying for the sick.

Two great contributions to medicine made by medieval monks stemmed from their skills at farming and at producing manuscripts. As they tended medieval gardens, monks became skilled at cultivating and using plants for medicinal remedies. They kept careful records of their work and their concoctions, thereby making their knowledge available for future generations. Some remedies combined plant medicinals with Christian rites and Germanic folk rituals. These remedies were intended to cure ail-

Monks and priests were among the most learned individuals in medieval society and were highly sought by the peasants for help in curing illness and injury.

ments caused by poisons, as well as possession by demons or other invisible forces.

REVIVING SCIENCE

The Renaissance (1300–1600) brought a return to the use of rational thought and scientific reasoning. Europeans began to seek a scientific basis for medical knowledge instead of relying on traditional meth-

MEDIEVAL DISEASES

The most notorious diseases of the Middle Ages were bubonic plague and leprosy. Bubonic plague was caused by infection with a bacterium transmitted by fleas. Symptoms included high fever, rash, and large, swollen lymph nodes, or buboes. In the late stages of the disease, bleeding under the skin turned it bluish black, giving rise to the term "black death." Today the disease can be treated with antibiotics; in the Middle Ages, however, infection caused death in about half of all cases. Plague was severely infectious and was responsible for devastating entire villages.

Leprosy, smallpox, and bubonic plague were among the most feared of medieval diseases. While some were lethal, others left debilitating and horrendous disfigurement.

Also greatly feared was leprosy, a disease caused by a bacterial infection and characterized by large painful sores all over the body, causing severe disfigurement. The disease was thought to be highly infectious. Lepers, as the infected were called, were forced to stay outside of towns, living in poorly-kept "leper houses" along main highways. Sometimes lepers were made to wear a bell so that healthy people would hear them coming. Today we know that leprosy is not highly contagious. It is completely curable with antibiotic therapy.

ods and the teachings of ancient physicians. It was a period marked by a renewed interest in the human body and people.

Loosening the ban on dissection was a major step forward in medical knowledge, allowing many physicians and some artists to closely examine the body and to record their observations in exquisite detail. Leonardo da Vinci dissected over thirty corpses in his study of human anatomy. His accurate anatomical diagrams deftly merged art with science. In 1543, the Flemish physician Andreas Vesalius published *De humani corporis fabrica libri septem* ("Seven Books on the Structure of the Human Body"), the most accurate work on human anatomy up to that time. Based on his careful and painstaking dissections of cadavers, the book laid the foundation for modern physiology.

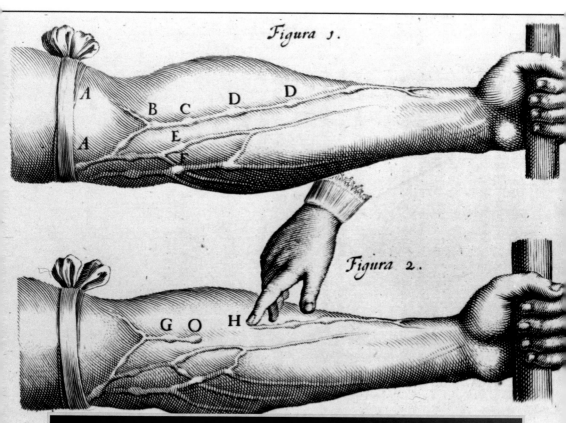

William Harvey's diagrams of blood vessels were instrumental to our modern understanding of the pathways of the human circulatory system.

Toward the end of the Renaissance, scientific innovations became more frequent. The printing press, developed in the mid-fifteenth century, had taken Europe by storm, making religious, literary, and scientific texts readily available to the upper classes. With the spread of ideas came a renewed search for more knowledge.

Chapter 3

A TURNING POINT FOR MEDICINE

By the sixteenth century, physicians had begun to apply a systematic approach to their studies of the body. Inspired by the new machines and tools of the Industrial Revolution that were used in manufacturing, physicians began to think less like philosophers and more like scientists in understanding and healing the body.

THE RISE OF THE MICROSCOPE

Three Dutch spectacle makers—Hans Jansen, his son Zacharias Jansen, and Hans Lippershey—have been credited with inventing the microscope around 1590. The first microscopes were simple devices made of wood, with an eyepiece and an objective lens. In the mid-1600s, the Dutch microscopist Anthony van

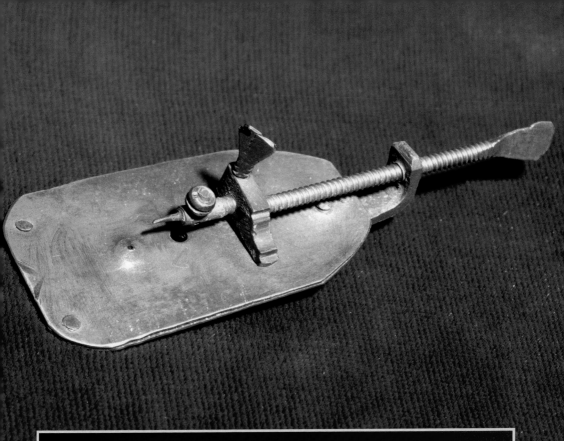

Early microscopes, such as the Leeuwenhoek microscope, were simple devices that relied upon basic mechanics and a separate light source.

Leeuwenhoek, produced improved lenses powerful enough to observe single-celled, animal-like creatures (protozoa) invisible to the naked eye.

The development of the microscope in the seventeenth century generated an explosion of interest in biological studies. The value of this important new research tool was phenomenal. Unsuspected processes and organisms unknown to science were discovered in a flurry of biological investigation. The concept of cells was introduced in 1665, when the English physicist Robert Hooke reported on the presence of tiny compartments in tissue he was studying under a microscope. Hooke named the compartments "cells."

The mystery of blood circulation within the body had long stumped physicians. Based on detailed and painstaking observations of his own veins and study of the blood vessels of sheep, English physician William Harvey determined that blood was pumped away from the heart via the arteries and was returned to it by way of the veins. Groundbreaking as this discovery was, however, Harvey could not explain how blood passed from the arteries to the veins.

Four years after Harvey's death in 1657, the Italian researcher Marcello Malpighi, with the aid of a microscope, identified and described the pulmonary and capillary networks that connected small arteries with small veins, solving Harvey's problem. Malpighi used the microscope to observe and describe many microscopic structures, including red blood cells. These discoveries provided critical information that enabled the English physician Richard Lower in 1665 to perform the first successful blood transfusion on dogs.

THE INFLUENCE OF THE INDUSTRIAL REVOLUTION

The Industrial Revolution (1760–1840) was a time noted for progress in many walks of life. The use of machines to do work previously performed by human labor called for an understanding of systems, an approach that was gradually incorporated into the study of the human body and the ailments that plagued it. This brought a growing interest in scientific investigation and invention.

The Industrial Revolution was an age of rapid mechanical progress and steady invention. The steam engine was put to work in a variety of ventures.

(continued on the next page)

31

(continued from the previous page)

However, though technology and science appeared to coevolve during the period, the relationship between them was not that straightforward. Early technology was based on hands-on experience rather than on science. Science had been the domain of the philosopher, while technology was in the hands of the craftsman. The two were not brought together until the sixteenth century when the English philosopher Francis Bacon suggested that scientists should study the methods of craftsmen and that craftsmen should understand more science.

THE FIRST VACCINES

Science and technology continued to evolve in the eighteenth century, where they helped bring relief from one of the most dreaded diseases: smallpox. The scourge of centuries, smallpox was a usually fatal disease that left those who survived greatly weakened and hideously scarred. When late in the eighteenth century Edward Jenner startled the medical profession by claiming that he had found a way to prevent smallpox infection, his claim was widely scorned.

Jenner had noticed that women who milked cows often caught cowpox, a relatively mild disease of cows, but they never developed the more virulent human disease smallpox. This observation led Jenner to wonder if variolation with cowpox could be used to prevent infection with smallpox. The practice of variolation then in use involved immunizing patients against smallpox by infecting them with material from the pustules of patients with a mild form of smallpox. The disease then usually occurred in a less-dangerous form than when contracted naturally. The method had long been known by the Turks and the Chinese, as well as other peoples, and had been practiced in England around 1721 by an English noblewoman, Lady Mary Wortley Montagu.

A major flaw in the method was that the transmitted disease sometimes converted to the virulent form. Furthermore, the inoculated person could disseminate the disease to others. In 1842, an act of Parliament in England made the practice of variolation a felony.

However, Jenner was convinced that variolation using cowpox instead of smallpox would confer immunity against the latter with fewer risks. He began developing what would become the world's

Lady Mary Wortley Montagu was an active proponent of smallpox inoculation, an early forerunner of the smallpox vaccine that eventually led to worldwide eradication of this devastating disease.

first vaccine against a virulent infectious disease. In 1796, he inoculated a young boy who had never had smallpox with material taken from cowpox lesions on the hands of a dairymaid. Several weeks later, he exposed the boy to smallpox. The boy remained healthy. Jenner wrote a scientific paper explaining his discovery, but it was received coldly in medical circles. Some years later, however, a London physician successfully vaccinated a patient using Jenner's method. This led to widespread acceptance of the method, which was later adapted to fight against many diseases.

Chapter 4

TECHNOLOGICAL REVOLUTION

Innovation continued to expand throughout the nineteenth century, and indeed the period from 1860 to 1914 is often called the Second Industrial Revolution. New scientific knowledge was applied to industry as scientists and engineers unlocked the secrets of physics and chemistry. These advances spurred development of mammoth industries, most notably steel, petroleum, chemicals, electricity, and transportation. The rise of these industries and the technology they inspired would have a tremendous impact on the advancement of medicine.

DISCOVERING GERMS

Certainly, one of the most important medical advances of the nineteenth century was the development and acceptance of the germ theory of disease, which proposed that certain diseases were caused by infection with microorganisms—organisms that are too small to be seen without a microscope. In the 1840s, Ignaz Semmelweis, a young physician working in a hospital in Vienna, recognized that doctors who performed autopsies and then delivered babies were responsible for spreading puerperal (childbed) fever, an often-deadly infection of the reproductive organs. After Semmelweis ordered doctors to wash their hands with a chlorinated lime solution before entering the maternity ward, deaths from puerperal fever plummeted.

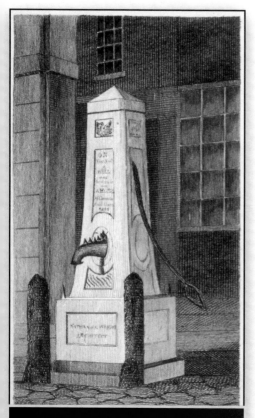

Dr. John Snow connected disease outbreaks to poor sanitation and water supply. His pivotal outbreak maps of London revealed that many were centered around local water pumps.

Another early pioneer in germ theory was John Snow, an English physician who documented the 1854 cholera outbreak in London, resulting in the closure of a neighborhood water pump that was spreading the disease. Snow reasoned that cholera was caused by a germ that was spread through contact with contaminated water, soiled clothing, and fecal matter. Snow used skilled reasoning, graphs, and maps to demonstrate the impact of the contaminated water coming from the water pump.

KILLER CONSUMPTION

As more people moved into cities and began to work at large factories, their close proximity and poor living conditions promoted the spread of many contagious diseases. Among the most deadly of these was tuberculosis, commonly known as consumption. The disease is caused by infection with *Mycobacterium tuberculosis*, a bacterium harbored in the respiratory system and spread when an infected person sneezes or coughs. Evidence suggests that tuberculosis infections occurred as many as nine thousand years ago. During the eighteenth and nineteenth centuries, tuberculosis reached near-epidemic proportions in the rapidly urbanizing and industrializing societies of Europe and North America. In fact, tuberculosis

(continued on the next page)

(continued from the previous page)

was the leading cause of death for all age groups in the Western world from that period until the early twentieth century, at which time improved health and hygiene brought about a steady decline in its mortality rates.

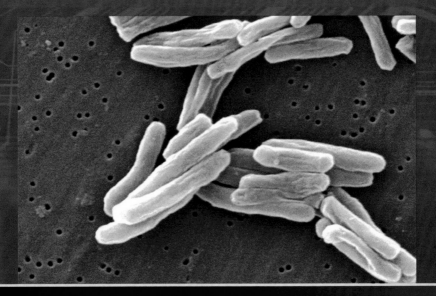

Mycobacterium tuberculosis was the culprit behind thousands of deaths into the twentieth century. When housed together in tight quarters, this air-and-fluid-borne bacteria quickly spread.

In France, chemist and microbiologist Louis Pasteur first learned about germs by studying the fermentation of beer, wine, and milk. Hearing of Pasteur's work, a local distiller came to him for help in controlling the process of making alcohol by fermenting beet sugar. Pasteur saw that fermentation was not a simple chemical reaction but took place only in the presence of living organisms. He learned that germs cause fermentation, putrefaction, infection, and souring. He went on to explore infectious diseases in farm animals and developed vaccines against anthrax in sheep, erysipelas in swine, chicken cholera in poultry, and rabies in humans.

Louis Pasteur was a driven and passionate scientist. Today, he is remembered as both a French hero and one of the most important founders of germ theory.

After reading Pasteur's studies, the British surgeon Joseph Lister theorized that germs could be transmitted by touch or by air, and were the cause for infection in wounds. He developed an antiseptic protocol for surgery that included hand-washing, cleaning of surgical instruments, and use of clean linens. As a result of his newly imposed rules, the number of post-surgical deaths decreased dramatically.

Further contributions to germ theory were made by German doctor Robert Koch, whose painstaking laboratory research demonstrated how specific microbes cause specific diseases. Koch's experimental methods for isolation, growth, and identification of bacteria led to a landmark discovery: specific types of bacteria resulted in specific diseases.

THE ACCIDENTAL DISCOVERY OF ANESTHESIA

The discovery of anesthesia resulted from a prank. In the early months of 1842 in Jefferson, Georgia, a number of young men saw a traveling medicine vendor demonstrate a new curiosity—nitrous oxide, better known as laughing gas. The young men observed that volunteers who inhaled this gas felt extremely exhilarated. The men asked their friend Crawford Long, a young surgeon, to hold a "nitrous oxide frolic" for them in his room. Since he had no nitrous oxide, Long gave them a different gas—ether. The gas had the desired effect, causing exhilaration and some euphoria. The young men became extremely rowdy and pommeled one another severely. Long noticed that none of them seemed to feel pain, however. He decided to experiment with ether in his surgical work.

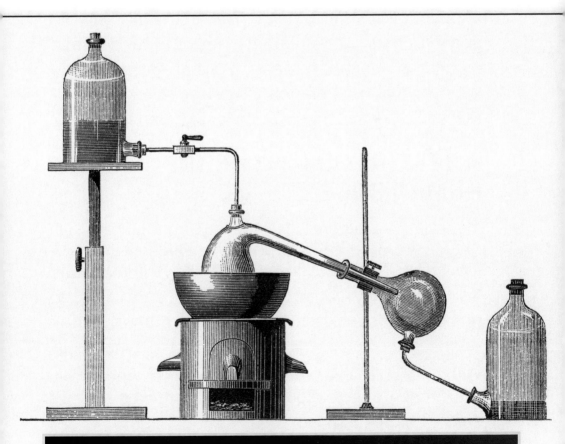

Ether's discovery heralded a new age of surgery for medical practices. Although intended for good, ether was also often abused as a recreational drug.

On March 30, 1842, Long performed what would be the first recorded surgical operation on an anesthetized patient. He administered sulfuric ether before removing a tumor from the neck of James Venable. The gas had the desired effect—Venable felt no pain during the surgery.

Despite the success of the procedure, Long was reluctant to publish his discovery until he had more experience with anesthesia. The first public demonstration of surgical anesthesia came in 1846, when another American surgeon, William Morton, used ether during an operation to remove a jaw tumor at Massachusetts General Hospital in Boston.

A BETTER LOOK INSIDE THE HUMAN BODY

It is hard to imagine modern medicine without the ability to take a look inside the human body. Yet surprisingly, a good deal of the technology that powers the equipment we take for granted today wasn't discovered until the end of the nineteenth century. As is often the case in science and medicine, much of this modern technology was discovered by happenstance.

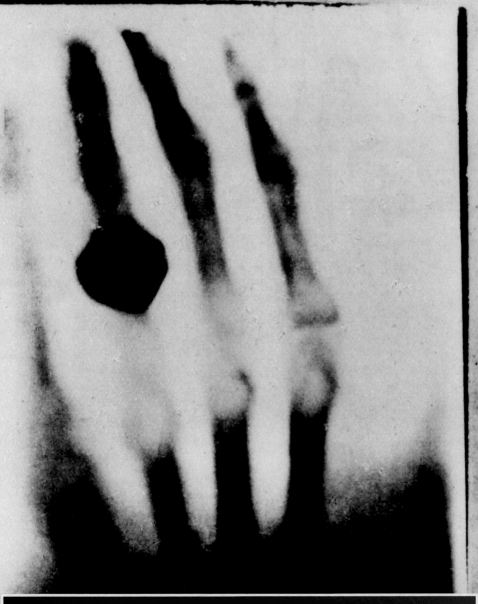

Radiographs of the human hand revealed a new way of looking inside the body to understand the relationships of bones, organs, and tissues.

An example of this is the radiograph, or X-ray. The X-ray was discovered during the course of research into the effects of high-voltage electricity on gases in 1895. A scientist named Wilhelm Conrad Roentgen discovered X-rays while working with cathode-ray tubes at his lab in Germany. Inside the tube was a gas that reacted to the positive and negative electrodes that were attached to the tube. Despite trying to shield the glow produced by putting a heavy black paper in front of the tube, Roentgen discovered the glow was still reacting—through the black paper—with other materials in the room. Roentgen reasoned that a new kind of light, or X-ray, was passing through the paper. He experimented with the X-ray, learning it could pass through some solid objects, including the human body. He took the first X-ray of the human body when he snapped a shot of the bones in his wife's hand.

Roentgen's discovery caused a great stir and led to the discovery of radioactivity. Sadly, it wasn't initially known that radiation could be harmful. In fact, many doctors and scientists believed that exposure to radiation could be beneficial to patients suffering from nervous diseases, constipation, or high blood pressure. It wasn't until Pierre and Marie Curie's work with radiation that its potential danger began to be acknowledged.

After the discovery of X-rays, there followed a flurry of medical discoveries that capitalized on the new technology. In the 1910s, chest X-rays became the diagnostic tool of choice for physicians who suspected tuberculosis in patients. The chest images allowed early detection of lung lesions in patients before they began to show clinical signs of the disease, allowing for earlier treatment. In 1919, Argentine physician Dr. Carlos Heuser was the first to use a contrast medium, potassium iodide, in a live subject to view the human circulatory system in action. Not long afterward, chest X-rays began to be used in the diagnosis and treatment of tuberculosis.

Chapter 5

MODERN MATERIALS

The twentieth century brought increased specialization in medicine as more technology became available to diagnose and heal medical conditions. Advanced imaging equipment such as ultrasound, MRIs, CT scanners, and electron microscopes became available. These, in combination with an ever-growing knowledge of the human body and the processes of disease, allowed for the development of ever more complex life-saving surgical and medical procedures.

THE BIRTH OF PHARMACOLOGY

Discoveries in pharmacology—the study of how medicines interact with the body—were among the most important medical advances of the twentieth century. The study of drugs stretches far back to ancient

Greece. The first Western pharmacological treatise, a listing of herbal plants used in classical medicine, was made in the first century CE by the Greek physician Dioscorides. The medical discipline of pharmacology derives from the medieval apothecaries, who both prepared and prescribed drugs. The field became formally established in the late nineteenth century thanks to the efforts of the German chemist Oswald Schmeiderberg, who defined its purpose, wrote a textbook of pharmacology, and established the first school for the formal study of pharmacology.

One of the greatest advances in medicine began with the discovery of the antibiotic penicillin in 1928 by the Scottish bacteriologist Alexander Fleming. While conducting research on bacteria, Fleming noticed that colonies of the bacterium *Staphylococcus aureus* would not grow near the green mold *Penicillium notatum*. He kept a strain of the mold alive and through testing determined that it produced a substance that was capable of killing many of the common bacteria that infect humans. The efforts of Fleming and others to extract enough pure concentrated penicillin to use in medicine were unsuccessful for many years. The drug eventually came into use during World War II as the result of the work of

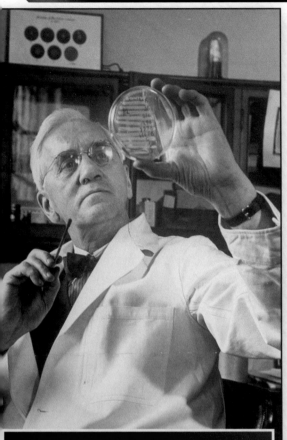

Alexander Fleming studied the growth of bacteria using agar-based petri dishes. Today, a variety of methods are used to identify and study bacteria.

a team of scientists led by Howard Florey and Ernst Chain at the University of Oxford. Hailed as the miracle drug of the twentieth century, penicillin saved millions of lives and paved the way for the development of countless other antibiotics.

The work of German electrical engineer Ernst Ruska contributed greatly to many fields of scientific study, from pharmacology to medicine to biochemistry. In the early 1930s, Ruska invented the electron microscope, so named because it directs a beam of electrons rather than light through a specimen. This technology allowed scientists for the first time to see the structures inside of cells, thereby opening a previously hidden world to medical knowledge and innovation.

DNA ROCKS THE WORLD

The discovery of deoxyribonucleic acid (DNA) would forever change the study of medicine and people. DNA is the material that makes up genes, the units of heredity. The information carried in DNA determines every inherited physical characteristic of every living thing. It controls how cells replicate and function and what traits are inherited from previous generations.

DNA was first discovered in 1869, but its structure and its role in genetics was not clear until the 1940s. Then, in 1953, scientists James Watson, Francis Crick, Maurice Wilkins, and Rosalind Franklin determined the double-helix structure of DNA, as well as its method of replication. Their work earned a Nobel Prize in 1962. Their discovery revealed for the first time how genetic traits are passed on from generation to generation.

However, knowing what DNA was did not explain exactly what it contained. Advances in the technology needed to study DNA at the molecular and cellular levels led to the determination of the scientific community to identify every human gene. In 1988, an international effort called the Human Genome Project was established with the goal to identify

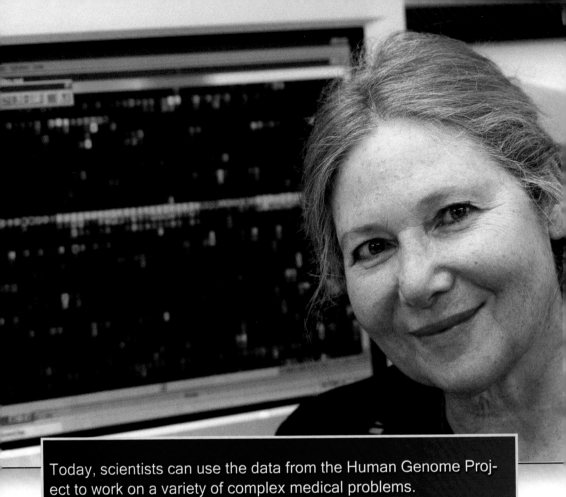

Today, scientists can use the data from the Human Genome Project to work on a variety of complex medical problems.

every human gene. It was one of the boldest scientific undertakings in history and one of the most successful. After thirteen years and the collaboration of more than 2,800 researchers, project officials announced that all human genes (about 22,000) had been identified. The genetic information provided by the project has enabled researchers to pinpoint errors in genes that cause or contribute to disease.

Having the tools to know the precise genetic makeup of individuals will enable clinicians to deliver truly personalized medicine.

COMPUTERS TRANSFORM PSYCHOLOGY

Psychology began as an experimental discipline and was eventually recognized as a scientific discipline. A key development in this evolution was the use of computers. Many psychological tests are now computerized. This approach allows for immediate scoring and processing. Using computers also makes it possible to compare a subject's response pattern to that of many others. As a result, immediate and accurate diagnoses are readily available.

Computers have also made psychological research more efficient and effective. With the aid of computer programs, the presentation of stimuli is more controllable than in the past. Computer programs also make it possible to deal with increasingly complex variables than was true when statistical analysis was limited to calculators.

IMPLANTS, PROSTHETICS, AND ASSISTIVE TECHNOLOGIES

Technological and engineering advances have fostered development of numerous devices that can be applied to medical problems. Some of these devices were assistive technologies, and they were central to the practice of medicine in the twentieth century. Assistive technologies are software or devices that help disabled people to move, see, hear, or use otherwise inaccessible facilities. Early assistive technologies included prostheses, external hearing aids, and ventilators.

Continued development of these technologies made it possible to devise prosthetic replacements for many of the body's major organs and tissues by means of surgical implantation. Faulty or blocked arteries and veins can now be replaced with tiny polyurethane tubes that carry blood to tissues and muscles. Weak heart valves can be replaced with special silicone substitutes. Electrodes implanted in the ear and connected magnetically to an external sound receiver can provide hearing to the profoundly deaf. Lenses of the eye that have been removed

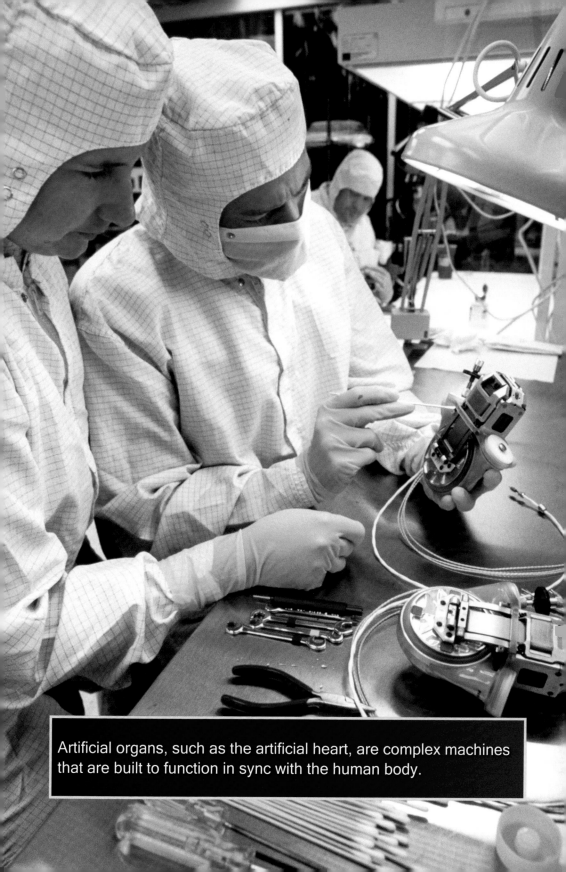

Artificial organs, such as the artificial heart, are complex machines that are built to function in sync with the human body.

during cataract surgery can be replaced with tiny intraocular lenses made of plastic.

Some prosthetic devices are used as temporary replacements for an affected organ. The heart-lung machine, which consists of an artificial lung, or oxygenator, and a substitute heart, or pump, is used during open-heart surgery. An implantable mechanical heart-assist device, the left-ventricular assist system, can act as a temporary substitute for the natural heart while patients wait for heart transplants. The dialysis machine is an external device that is used several times a week to purify the blood of patients suffering kidney damage or failure.

ORGAN TRANSPLANTS

With the advent of assistive technologies such as the artificial lung and the heart pump, vital organ transplants became possible. In 1967, South African surgeon Christiaan Barnard made medical history by performing the first human heart transplant. Although the surgery itself was successful, the patient died less than three weeks later of complications from pneumonia. Subsequent attempts at transplants performed by Barnard as well as other doctors failed also, largely because the patients' bodies rejected the implanted organ. In the 1970s cyclosporine, a compound isolated from an earth fungus, was discovered to be a very effective drug for combating rejection. Today it is widely used for transplant procedures, allowing for relatively good success rates.

In addition to transplants with human organs made available through donors, great progress has been made with the design and use of artificial organs. The development and construction of artificial organs and limbs is the focus of biomedical engineering. With the advent of computer-aided design (CAD) systems, biomedical engineers and orthopedic surgeons can design and build a prosthesis that is customized to an individual patient. 3D printers have enabled scientists to create artificial bone and base plates used in joint transplants and artificial limbs. Further advances in the field of bioengineering have also yielded 3D printers that can produce living tissue such as muscles, cartilage, and bone.

THE FUTURE OF MEDICINE

Those who want to practice medicine must meet educational, professional, and ethical standards

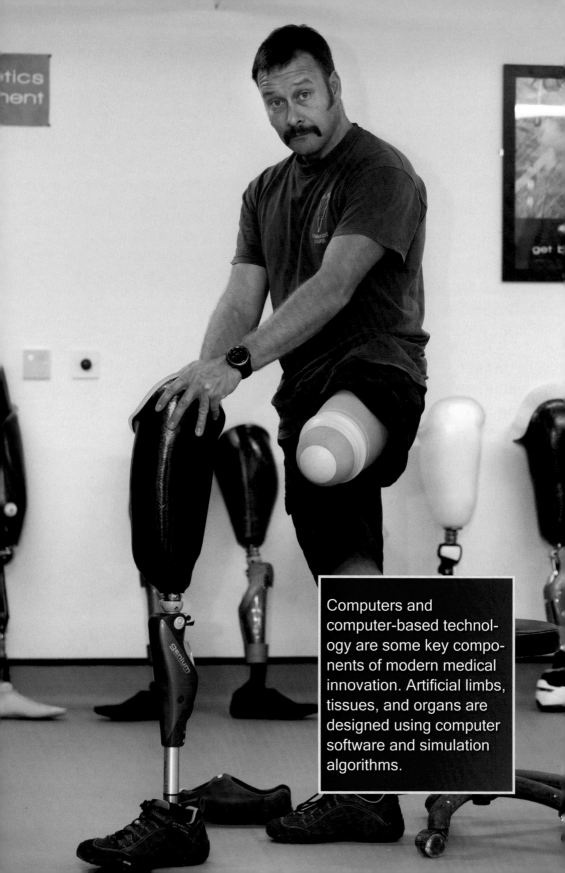

Computers and computer-based technology are some key components of modern medical innovation. Artificial limbs, tissues, and organs are designed using computer software and simulation algorithms.

before their state, province, or country awards them a license to treat patients. Approaches to medical education, licensing, and practice vary throughout the world.

Still, questions arise. Should scientists change the genetic information in bacteria, in animal species, and in plants? Physicians can keep seriously ill patients alive indefinitely, using artificial respirators, machines that take over the control of the beating of the heart, and drugs to control blood pressure and consciousness. But should they? And, should patients be able to choose to die?

Citizens are claiming "patients' rights," insisting on being informed about medical procedures, and deciding how to allocate health resources fairly. When they ask these questions and make these decisions, they are dealing with bioethics.

Religious groups have for centuries developed their own positions on many important bioethical issues. It is clear that as medicine and medical technology coevolve, they will likely clash with traditional ways of thinking unless medical professionals and religious or otherwise morally motivated groups come to some agreement.

GLOSSARY

ACUPUNCTURE The Chinese practice of inserting fine needles through the skin at specific points, especially to cure disease or relieve pain.

ANTISEPTIC A substance that prevents or arrests the growth of microorganisms.

BIOMEDICAL ENGINEERING Biological or medical application of engineering principles or engineering equipment.

CAPILLARY NETWORK A collection of slender hairlike tubes that are the smallest blood vessels, connecting arteries with veins.

CASE HISTORY A record of history, environment, and relevant details of a case.

CHOREA A movement disorder marked by involuntary spasmodic movements.

COMPOUND MICROSCOPE A microscope consisting of an objective and an eyepiece mounted in a drawtube. It uses multiple lenses to enlarge a sample.

COMPUTERTIZED TOMOGRAPHY (CT) Diagnostic imaging method using a low-dose beam of X-rays that crosses the body in a single plane at many different angles.

DIAGNOSIS The process of identifying a disease or medical condition.

DISEASE A condition of a living animal or plant body or of one of its parts that impairs normal functioning and is typically manifested by distinguishing signs and symptoms.

DISSECT To separate into pieces and expose the several parts of something, such as an animal for scientific examination.

ELECTRON MICROSCOPE An electron-optical instrument in which a beam of electrons is issued to produce an enlarged image of a minute object.

EPIDEMIOLOGY A branch of medical science that deals with the incidence, distribution, and control of disease in a population.

ERYSIPELAS An acute disease associated with intense inflammation of the skin and tissues.

HERNIA A protrusion of an organ or part through connective tissue or through the wall of a cavity.

INFIRMARY A place where sick or injured individuals receive care and treatment.

INOCULATE To introduce a microorganism into.

MAGNETIC RESONANCE IMAGING (MRI) A non-invasive diagnostic technique that produces computerized images of internal body tissues and is based on nuclear magnetic resonance of atoms within the body.

MORTALITY The quality or state of being able to die. Or, the rate of death in a group.

PULMONARY Of, relating to, affecting, or occurring in the lungs.

SCIENTIFIC METHOD Principles and procedures for the systematic pursuit of knowledge involving recognizing a problem, collecting data, and forming and testing hypotheses.

TRANSFUSION The process of transfusing or passing fluid (such as blood) into a vein or artery.

PROSTHESIS An artificial device to replace or augment a missing or impaired part of the body.

ULTRASOUND A noninvasive technique involving the formation of a two-dimensional image used for the examination and measurement of internal body structure or abnormalities.

FOR FURTHER READING

Aldridge, Susan. *Trailblazers in Medicine.* New York, NY: Rosen Young Adult, 2015.

Arnold, Nick. *Blood, Bones, and Body Bits.* London, UK: Scholastic, 2014.

Basher, Simon. *Basher Science: Extreme Biology: From Superbugs to Clones…Get to the Edge of Science.* New York, NY: Kingfisher, 2013.

Boring, Mel. *Guinea Pig Scientists: Bold Self-Experiments in Science and Medicine.* New York, NY: Square Fish, 2014.

Faust, Daniel. *Medical Robots.* New York, NY: PowerKids Press, 2016.

Green, Dan. *The Adventures of Your Brain.* New York, NY: Sterling Children's Books, 2017.

Ignotofsky, Rachel. *Women in Science: 50 Fearless Pioneers Who Changed the World.* New York, NY: Ten Speed Press, 2016.

Johnson, Rose. *Discoveries in Medicine that Changed the World.* New York, NY: Rosen Central, 2015.

Leavitt, Amie Jane. *Jump-Starting a Career in Medical Technology.* New York, NY: Rosen Young Adult, 2014.

Lim, Bridget. *Avicenna: Leading Physician and Philosopher-Scientist of the Islamic Golden Age.* New York, NY: Rosen Young Adult, 2016.

Medicine: The Definitive Illustrated History. New York, NY: DK, 2016.

Rooney, Anne. *The History of Medicine.* New York, NY: Rosen Publishing, 2013.

Veasey, Nick. *X-Ray: See Through the World Around You.* New York, NY: Goodman, 2013.

WEBSITES

Lens on Leeuwenhoek
https://lensonleeuwenhoek.net/

New York Times
http://www.nytimes.com/interactive/2012/10/05/health/digital-doctor.html#/#time15_331
Twitter, Facebook, Instagram: @nytimes

Science Daily - Medical Technology News
https://www.sciencedaily.com/news/matter_energy/medical_technology/

INDEX